Noise of the World

Noise of the World

George Franklin

Sheila-Na-Gig Editions

Volume 7

Author photo: © Ximena Gómez
Cover art: Paul Cézanne, *The Basket of Apples*, 1893, oil on canvas

ISBN: 978-1-7354002-0-4
Library of Congress Control Number: 2020943408

Published by Sheila-Na-Gig Editions
Russell, KY
www.sheilanagigblog.com

For Ximena,

Mi compañera y mi amor.

ACKNOWLEDGMENTS

Many thanks to the editors and staff of the following journals in which these poems have appeared:

Barely South Review: "Pink Neon in North Louisiana," "Sightseeing"
Black Coffee Review: "Falling."
Cagibi: "Friday," "La Casa de los Azulejos," "This Week"
Chaleur: "Are You Jewish?" "Danse Macabre"
Cider Press Review: "While I Slept"
Into the Void: "Elegy" "Treatment"
La Libélula Vaga: "Lunch with Kafka," "Treatment"
Matter: a (somewhat) monthly journal of political poetry and commentary: "Brodsky in New York," "Miami Beach Prepares for Climate Change," "New Year's Day," "San Antonio," "Vallejo in Paris"
Nagari: "A Friend Writes," "Are You Jewish," "Lunch with Kafka"
Ocotillo Review: "Later On"
Sheila-Na-Gig Online: "An Hour South of Cali," "Breaking Curfew," "Clean Sheets," "Crivelli's Madonna and Child," "Desire," "Eurydice," "Knossos," "In Retrospect," "Noise of the World," "Notre-Dame de Paris," "Of Almost Savage Torpor," "Pneumonia," "Scritch-Scratch," "The Detention Camp at Pisa, 1945," "The Syllabus," "The Winter Ducks"
Panoply: A Literary Zine: "Kitsch"
The American Journal of Poetry: "A fairer House than Prose"
The Blue Nib: "Hiding," "When Love Is Hard to Talk About"
The Ekphrastic Review: "Falling Apart," and "Caravaggio," (appearing under the title "You Asked for an Example of Realism")
The Ghazal Page: "Ghazal"
The Ilanot Review: "Ghazal of Puebla"
The Lake: "In Our Stories," "Pieter Bruegel the Elder Looks at Two Monkeys," "Quarantine Days"
The Pedestal Magazine: "Reverie"
The Wild Word: "Agua," "Caffè Corretto," "Yellow Peaches from Chile"
Twyckenham Notes: "October"
Typishly: "Nowhere"
Verse-Virtual: "A Friend Writes," "Agua," "Knossos"

Special thanks to *Broadsided Press*, for publishing "Shreveport" as a broadside, and to the judges of the 2020 Stephen A. DiBiase Poetry Prize for choosing "Agua" as the first-place winner.

CONTENTS

III. "A fairer House than Prose"

IV. The Winter Ducks

V. Noise of the World

Falling Apart

On my table tonight in a bowl, apples and pears,
Balanced against each other, stem to glossy skin.
If they are joined at all, it's an intricate architecture,
Forces at rest. It makes me think of Cézanne
And his basket of apples spilling out onto the table,
The wine bottle leaning like the Tower of Pisa in
Miniature, folds of the towel forming ski slopes
For apples, the disjointed table, and toasted
Biscuits stacked crossways on the white plate—
The world seems to be falling apart, held together
Only for a moment by the frame of the painting.
It is Poussin's *L'Enlèvement des Sabines* enacted
By a basket of apples, by biscuits and a white plate,
And underneath the plate, barely noticed, lies a
Notebook, level, undisturbed.

I.

Agua

AGUA

Am I any closer to knowing you here, where you grew up—
One of three sisters, like in Chekhov—in a valley hugging
The Cauca River, mountains blue as rain in the distance?

Upstairs at the nursing home, your father grows thinner,
And you give him water by the spoonful, so he won't choke. He
Calls you *mijita* and asks you to close the window. His

Face has shrunk to bones and cartilage. His eyes are large and
Searching. There are neighborhoods in Cali where you walked,
Looking at birds and bougainvillea, the impenetrable green

Of the future. We haven't had time to see the places you lived,
For you to tell me what you fantasized as you stepped over
Cracks in the sidewalk, dodged traffic. The first days we were

Here, your father learned my name, but now he's forgotten it.
He thinks I'm "Jaime" and can't be convinced otherwise. Will
We all end up like this? In the garden below, there are birdsongs

I don't recognize, but plants that I do: heliconia and bird of
Paradise, ginger blossoms red as candy and that kind of ginger
With the white blossoms too. Yesterday, there was a huge cat

Observing everything, and a turtle that stopped to look at me
Reading, then strolled off, scratching his small black nails
Against the concrete. I didn't get a chance to introduce myself.

When you leave the place you were raised, it ceases to exist, and
You cease to exist in the same way. The signs are changed
Above the shops, the highways become more crowded. Now,

Everyone has motorcycles. I imagine you reading Freud in
That massive library or maybe Spinoza, your thoughts drifting
To coffee and dancing salsa with your friends, or listening to

Estanislao Zuleta disparage his contemporaries. How far is it
From Colombia to Miami, to your apartment in Midtown, to
Translating the narratives of immigrants asking for asylum—

Venezuelans who don't want to be sent back to die or
To beg in the streets of Cali or some other place? Yesterday,
We saw families by the side of the road to Pance, with nothing,

Stopping here or headed farther south. Men with cardboard signs
At the intersections, asking for pesos. But, none of this brings me
Closer to you. At night in our room, we touch each other, carefully,

And then with hunger, fingers and mouths unrestrained, thighs open,
Looking for what? I've never figured this out. The room smells
Vaguely of cigarettes, but we're showered, our skin damp and cool.

Your father is probably dozing. There is not much left you can say
To him now. The water you give him is a kind of sacrament,
A way of preparing for a time when preparation doesn't matter,

Preparing you for continuing. When you leave, he will cease to
Exist, and you will also in the way you existed before.
His wrists and hands are transparent. He reaches for the cup you

Can't give him. You remind him, one spoon, then another.
He gags, coughs, swallows the fluids that fill his throat, takes
A shallow breath, asks for more water. Tomorrow, we will fly back

To Miami. The residents of the home will be eating dinner, watching
Television, voices, music in the background, unaffected by the heat,
The mosquitoes that come around in the evening. Your father will

Lie in bed, waiting for sleep to cover him, his mouth dry. On the plane,
I'll touch your hand, then bring it to my lips. *Forgive me, mi amor, for
Knowing so little, for not even knowing what it is I want to know.*

PNEUMONIA

A message from Colombia last night — your
Father had been moved to the hospital again,
For pneumonia this time, his lungs thick

With phlegm, his skin almost transparent.
When we visited a few weeks past, he
Could still talk a little, huddled beneath

Blankets and sheets. It was summer there,
And he was always thirsty. I kept wondering
When it would be too much for you — you knew

He was dying, his legs as thin as your wrists,
Face gaunt. I remembered how my own father
Looked at the end, how his skull seemed to

Be poking up through his face, how his eyes
Seemed larger than before. There wasn't much
You could do for him, just as there was nothing

I'd been able to do for my father, except to
Bring him home, let him die without doctors
And monitors, without the machinery that

Pretends death won't happen, until it does.
I'm sorry we can't do that for your father as well,
Take him back to the house where you grew up —

Gone now, windows boarded, yard unkept —
Take him back there to a room where he could
Look out at mountains, cresting green and steep,

To the west, the north. Somewhere out there, a river
Slides south toward Ecuador and the Andes, and
If it's morning, the sun will be rising over trees

And livestock—those horses we saw grazing in
Fields alongside the cattle. Downstairs, the daily
Sounds of someone fixing breakfast, of plates and

Silverware, and the smell of hot milk and coffee,
Of eggs and freshly baked rolls. But, we can't
Do that now. The best we can hope for him is sleep,

A few breaths, dry and open, a nurse touching his
Hand. Memory itself may already have gone dark,
Turned off its shop signs, pulled down the gates.

When we spoke, you mentioned "The Death of
Ivan Ilych," and I thought about how much he
Wanted to understand and about what couldn't

Be understood. It seems to me that a man's death
Is not his own. It doesn't belong to him. It's
Not his to understand. It belongs to the ones who

Love him and the people who love them. It
Stretches like a wool blanket over cold thin legs or
A night sky, remote, over the mountains.

FUNERAL

Last night when we got home, the big dipper
Was directly overhead. I pointed it out to you and
Tried to find the north star. Maybe I was right,

Maybe not. The city lights made it hard to see.
The trip to Cali had been hard in a different way.
We got there just in time for your father's

Funeral, stood beside his coffin with the rest of
Your family. He was ninety-one and had outlived
Friends, your mother too. When they lifted

The lid, I could see his face had color again—
Make-up, of course—but he wasn't there. I thought,
He's a ghost now—not the kind that rattles

Dishes in a cupboard but an emptiness
Making the world feel colder and strange,
Not a missing person but a person missing.

Outside the wooden door with your father's name
On a placard, other families walked by, going to
Or from their own wood-paneled rooms and doors.

In one, I'd seen three women and a man, motionless,
Staring at the hole that had just been cut in their lives,
In another, a larger family chatting, uncomfortable,

Unable to stand or sit still. After a while, a young
Woman with an official air came in and read a short
Speech in Spanish that I didn't understand, and

Dark-haired men in white shirts moved your father
Efficiently to a hearse in the garage, from there
To a cemetery in the mountains.

*

The next day, we bought fruit at Galería Alameda
And taxied from San Antonio to see places
You'd lived growing up, the house your father

Bought by the Río Cali—it's a business now, but the
Security guard let us in to look around, see
Your old kitchen, the terrazzo floors, the room

Where you studied. Later, we went out for coffee,
And pastries, did the things people do to
Remind themselves they're still alive.

*

On the flight back, we read poems by Primo Levi.
There was an empty seat next to us,
And you slept with your head in my lap.

An Hour South of Cali

On the road, five horses, riders in high
Boots, polo shirts—our taxi pulls over to let
Them go by. The white walls are high and thick

To keep out intruders. Vines grow wildly
Over the top—blue flowers I haven't seen before.
At the gate to the nursing home, you ring

The bell and wait. Eventually, a young woman
Arrives and lets us in. We learn later she
Is Venezuelan. Her *novio* is a taxi driver,

And he picks her up at the end of her shift.
He also brings her energy drinks that are
Sold on the side of the highway. We went

There every day to see your father. While you
Tended to him—the air in his room stagnant
With heat, the window closed—I sat downstairs

In the shade, reading Orwell's Homage to
Catalonia. His Barcelona where everyone was
Equal gave way, one street at a time, betrayed

By Stalinists and Republicans alike. Orwell
Left, hunted by the police, and never came back,
Died of tuberculosis, coughing the way

I could hear your father cough upstairs, gagging
On water, a spoonful of yogurt. On the other
Side of the walls, there are still green fields,

Cattle, a river to the west, ranches, and groups
Of elegant houses with gates and guards.
The horses pass, hooves clattering on the pavement.

Yellow Peaches from Chile

In the parking lot of Whole Foods, the women's blouses are the colors
of carnations and marigolds. They hold the hands of their
distracted children, guide their shopping carts toward cars whose
trunks pop open with the press of a pink thumbnail against a key.

Holding grocery bags in both hands, the men wear black t-shirts as
though it's a political statement. They close the tailgates of their
SUVs with measured force, and dark glasses dangle from their
necks like relics.

A brown-haired woman in a green apron speaks Spanish to her
daughter on a cell phone. Her shift won't be over for three more
hours. Someone calls her to come to the grocery aisle by the
applesauce. She gets up, takes a deep breath, goes back inside.

I notice that there are five different kinds of bananas over by the
potatoes and the onions.

Who buys all this cheese?

At the olive bar, I see those little red peppers that are sweet and hot at
the same time. I had them on pizza once in Arlington, Virginia.

At the supplements and soaps, the sales assistant has purple hair.
Where, someone asks, is the acidophilus?

It's hard to leave without buying something, so I settle on a muffin
and coffee, taking it outside to look at the afternoon sky, the white
half-moon visible in daylight.

I break the muffin in half and take bites in between sips of coffee.
Why is it so difficult to remember that none of us live forever?

GHAZAL

At night beneath mosquito netting, we'd lie in the garden—
Beneath my hands and lips your body, a garden within a garden.

By wilted roses, I kissed your breasts and believed I would hear
Nightingales, but there were no birds in the garden.

Even at this hour, you can hear the passing traffic. I listen
For footsteps on the walkway, but who'd visit an empty garden?

There are office buildings and apartments all along the street,
A billboard advertising Japanese motorcycles, parked in a garden.

I look for the oldest man I can find and ask him, "Over there,
Didn't there used to be a garden?"

He shakes his head, laughs with missing teeth. "You're confused.
I've lived here all my life. There was never a garden."

WHEN LOVE IS HARD TO TALK ABOUT

I made *ceviche de pescado*
This weekend as a surprise for you,

Cutting corvina into cold, white
Slices, fish you could almost see through,

Marinated in lime and coarse salt,
In onions, cilantro, mangos too.

I boiled sweet potatoes, stir-fried the
Corn—you teased me because I had two

Servings, thought about more. I'm happy,
but also frightened when I'm with you,

Worried that I'll screw it up somehow.
Before we met, I'd learned to make do,

Asked myself, "Why the hurry? It takes
Twenty years to fail at something new."

Your Side of the Bed

When you're not here, I wake up at odd
Angles, my legs flung to your side of
The bed. The blanket must have been too
Warm or too cool, and my legs had gone
Looking for you while I slept badly,
Dreaming I'd lost a child in a white
Dress. A freight elevator carried
Me from floor to floor as I looked for
Her — without result. When you're not here,
That television screen behind my
Eyelids oscillates images of
Loss, celadon vases broken in
Sharp fragments, wooden splinters gouged
From my old desk, important papers
Torn away by a malicious wind.

When you're not here, I can sleep any
Way that appeals to me. I can put
My head beneath your pillows to feel
How cool they are and dark. I can keep
My eyes open to see the sliver
Of blue light from my cellphone. If it's
Already dawn outside, I can turn
Away from the window shades that cut
The morning into shadows, lines, and
Rectangles. I can turn, with eyes closed,
Toward your hair, your shoulders lifting and
Falling with your breath. I can throw my
Legs in front of me, pull the sheets up,
And push myself back into sleep, where
I can almost forget you're not here.

LATER ON

This evening, I found one of your hairs
On a napkin beside the honey.
I imagine you at breakfast as
You lift the plastic bear, flip the lid,
And squeeze drops of honey into your
Coffee cup, hands a little sticky,
Touching your brown hair, then the napkin.
How much of us we leave behind, these
Random pieces of our lives, ourselves.
I left early this morning, didn't
Have time to sit with you, bring your hand
To my lips, honey on your fingers.

How to Cook a Frittata

Begin with what you have already,
Yesterday's sockeye salmon—take off
The skin and give it to the dog who
Sits looking at you—asparagus,
Barely cooked and bright green, an onion
The largest one you've got, chopped till your
Eyes water. Ask the woman standing
Next to you in the kitchen, the one
Who is patient and a better cook
Than you, to add salt to the eggs—you
Would put in too much or too little.
Then, heat olive oil, the kind that smells
Like that field in Torcello with the
Trees bent over, gnarled. The pan should be
Old and scratched, cast iron or something
You inherited. Nothing non-stick
Or perfect. This is not about slick
Or slippery. If you do it right,
There will be brown bits of egg you have
To scrape off the pan at the end, but
We're not there yet. You'll wait for the oil
To bubble, and you'll stir in onions
And some herbs. Anything else like some
Left-over potatoes, or pasta—
Add it now, as you drink wine from a
Juice glass or even a cup. Careful
Adding the salmon, asparagus,
And then the eggs. The pan will be full
And you don't want the eggs to burn on
The bottom. Parmesan cheese covers
The top, and then under the broiler
As you watch it turn crusty and gold.
Pour some more wine for you both and eat.

DESIRE

The café is closing soon, and I've
Been reading about desire, which seems
Useless. Grammar has nothing to do

With what pushes inchoate from the
Inside. We pretend to be circus
Performers, juggling strings of words like

Bright bowling pins, spinning awkwardly
Back to our hands. I write, *I want you,*
Without any idea what that

Means, like saying *we give ourselves to
Each other*, allowing desire to
Run down our thighs like warm water, or

Pressing my lips and teeth hard against
Your shoulder, dissolving beneath your
Fingers, tongue, the shiver in your

Abdomen? No part of speech fits then.
How embarrassing if the people
At the next table, the family

Finishing their sandwiches and drinks,
Knew what I'm thinking, waiting for you,
My head turned toward the evening traffic.

CLEAN SHEETS

I just made the bed with clean sheets. They're
Wrinkled but washed and fresh smelling, the
Weave a little rough against my hands.
When you get here, I'll fix coffee, yours
With steamed milk, foamy, mine dark,
Tasting of burnt sugar, reminding
Me of the night sky in another
Latitude, that neighborhood where we,
Walked, the moon still not up over the
Hills, the low rooftops, hotel signs, and
Shuttered windows, from somewhere voices,
Music, a dog barking behind a
High white wall, my lips touching your neck.
After dinner, we'll turn back the sheets,
Slip in beside each other, our days
Still with us, scents we can't get rid of,
Sandalwood clinging to your nightgown,
Lemon peel, onions on my fingers.
When we touch, we could be anywhere.

If You Ask

If you ask me whether these
Sheets exist, I'll tell you they
Do, and your skin exists as
Well, your lips and teeth holding
My lips, my teeth pressing back,
Biting your neck and shoulder,
Your nipples turning hard as
My mouth moves over them, the
Smooth white flesh of your thighs and
Calves—all that exists too. But,
Whoever I was before
We touched each other doesn't.

THE SIMPLEST POEM I KNOW HOW TO WRITE

Each day, it takes me longer to get back into the world,
Sleep more reluctant to let go, my back stiff, throat congested,
My legs learning to walk all over again, the balls of my feet
Trying to find the floor in just the right way. If I sit for a moment,
I can tell sleep is still looking for me. Thoughts slide up
Against each other, tell stories that don't make any sense. Eyelids
Flutter like a broken television, the picture refusing to stay in place.

Each day, it takes me longer to get back into the world,
When you're here, it's better, though I can't explain why.
I'll come back to bed and kiss your shoulder a few times, let my head
Rest next to you so I can smell your hair and feel the untroubled
Movement of your breath. You always ask what time it is, and I always
Check the clock, so that I can give you a precise and probably unnecessary
Answer. Then, it's time to get up again, go to make the coffee.

EURYDICE

I'm always afraid I'll turn around to find you gone,
Eurydice in a flowered dress, oversized bag on your shoulder,
Fading back into the lobby of your building, elevator retreating

Up to the tenth floor—you swallowed by the hallway
And the door, as afternoon light fades over the railroad tracks,
The graffitied buildings to the west. But, I'm not Orpheus,

And you're very much alive. In Colombia, the day after
Your father's funeral, we walked between the tables of a market,
Where you warned me in a serious voice to bury my cell phone

Deep in my front pocket to fend off thieves. But there weren't
Any thieves—Or at least we didn't see them—just piles of
Ripe berries, plantains, and yellow granadilla opening

To sweet gray flesh and black seeds. How long were we there,
Sampling mangos, staring at straw baskets, meat hanging
From iron hooks? Persephone ate six pomegranate seeds

And for eternity sits by Hades' side for half the year.
She was the one who begged her husband to let Eurydice leave,
Orpheus's song still echoing from those walls where the dead,

Having drunk from Lethe, forget the bright world and sleep.
When we emerged, your bag heavy with fruit, the sun was still
At the sky's center, the season unchanged, the traffic thick

With taxis and trucks, with motorcycles and those jeeps that
Carry passengers to the places taxis won't go. There were televisions
In shop windows, cars for sale on credit, billboards with bottles

Of tequila and aguardiente. Later, in our hotel room, we showered
Off the sweat and held each other. If I were Orpheus,
I would have looked back even sooner. In Miami,

I take your hand as we walk at night along Biscayne, clouds
Reflecting the city's light as they move east, out over the bay.
Only by touching do we know we're still here.

II.

Ghosts

GHOSTS

They are the same as they've ever been,
Getting up in the morning, going

To the closet for a shirt and pants,
Making coffee in the dark kitchen,

Sitting at the table as though there
Were a newspaper folded neatly

By the missing plate. They are the same
As ever, but no one notices.

Glamor

Up until he had a stroke, I walked
Each evening with my grandfather. He

Wore white suits to work in summer and
Ties handmade from Chinese silk. Twilight

Rolled downhill like something lost, and I'd
Listen to stories he'd make up or

Reprise from Shakespeare or Ibsen. Oak
Trees stretched over the street, and the cars

Were just starting to turn on their lights.
Later, he walked alone in the house

In his underwear and once slapped me
Hard at dinner for some imagined

Offense. My parents hired a man in
A flannel shirt to sit in the room

All night in case he needed something
Or he died in his sleep. I don't think

My mother wanted to be the one
To find him like that. But the man drank

Vodka when no one was looking, and
Was found sleeping peacefully on the

Couch. My father fired him and hired a
Distant relative who didn't drink.

*

In the house, there was a metal stand
That held a black walking stick with an

Ivory handle and a gold ring.
I took it before the estate sale,

And I kept it for years, pointlessly.

JUST ONCE

Just once, my father told this story.
He and his twin brother and his best
Friend crept out the back door of the house
To watch a hanging. He didn't say
Who the man was, whether he was white
Or black, whether it was a lynching
Or whether the sheriff held the rope—
Only that his parents told him he
Couldn't go, and when he got home, his
Father whipped him. He didn't say
What he'd felt when he learned how easy
It is to break a man's neck, how the
Bowels empty and the body jerks.
My father grew up a good man. He
Wasn't violent and wept watching
President Kennedy's funeral.
I don't know how often he thought back
To that hanging in Little Rock or
If he'd been frightened, excited, sad,
Or just too far back in the raucous
Crowd to see what happened. During the
Terror in France, barefoot children ran
To follow the carts to the scaffold
And chewed on apples as severed heads
Dropped into well-placed woven baskets.
Their parents might well have been there too.
Good people often have stood and watched
While a woman, screaming, was bound to
A post, nose and ears cut off, then stoned,
Or a man was cut in half, then cut
In half again. Did simple boredom
Bring them to the village square, the oak
Tree outside of town, Newgate Prison?
I wonder if my father climbed a
Lamppost to get a better view, or
Did he slip away and throw up in
The bushes where no one could see him?

SHREVEPORT

Every fence is an infinite line, a weave
Of intersections, a geometry workbook covered

With badly-drawn circles. Note to self: I
Hate this class. Staring out the louvered window,

Terra cotta tiles, the rooftop of a church
Across the street, green-speckled trees

By the sidewalk, the fried chicken sign,
Colonel Sanders also across the street—

I was too young even to drive, but I wanted to
Leave more than anything. A bottle of formaldehyde

Had smashed on the staircase. We all tried
To hold our breaths, walking from one class to another.

Every fence leads me back to that one by the
Football field and the track. There was a Chinese

Restaurant that stayed open late downtown.
I planned to go there for chow mein and won-tons

After my parents had fallen asleep. No one could
Convince me geometry was anything but a way

To build prisons. I wanted to be Jean-Paul Sartre,
But I was born on the wrong side of the Atlantic

And didn't speak French. We watched Vietnam
During breakfast on a black and white television,

Soldiers, rifle fire, narrow streets and motorcycles,
Newscasters' gray-white faces, black-rimmed glasses.

The fences reached there too.

Nowhere

All the losses we never knew we
Had clamber up our ribcages, sure-
Footed as only grief can be. We
Stretch out adolescent bodies on
Swings in the park, humid nights growing
Black around our movements, arms loosely
Holding onto the chains as we fly
Toward becoming someone else, adults
We won't recognize in the mirror.
Below, empty beer cans lie on the
Grass in a random pattern, like the
Sticks Chinese fortunetellers used to
Find a hexagram in the *I Ching*.
We all had futures, some shorter and
Sadder than others. There was a girl
Who died young. I don't know from what. She
Wrote poems she never showed me or
Anyone else. We made out once by
Cross Lake, getting high and avoiding
Cottonmouths rustling in the bushes.
She was busted a couple of nights
Later. I managed to get away
Just in time and watched the arrest
From behind a tree, afraid to move.
I took a taxi home and crawled in
Through a window. The police knew I'd
Been there but didn't have enough to
Pull me in. I don't know how many
Other times I got lucky. Friends did
Time in Angola or Huntsville in
Texas. I went to college up north,
Then to Britain and France, walking
Through the stone basement at the Louvre
In the morning with no one around,
Just me and the Assyrian gods,
Buying new clothes, books of poetry,

Taking the train to Edinburgh,
Where I lived above a Scottish pub,
A Dusty Springfield imitator
Singing loudly till I fell asleep.
When I got back, my friends all said I'd
Lost my Louisiana accent.
I sounded like someone from nowhere.

Pink Neon in North Louisiana

The Fina station on the road to the airport
Glowed in the dark like a shrine
To the god of petroleum. Sometimes,

We watched the planes come in low
Over the fence, their landing gear and
Tires practically parting our hair.

Denny's served Kona coffee and
Pie everyone said wasn't half bad. There
Are drive-through daquiri shops now

Where barbeque pits used to smoke all night.
The Carousel Lounge on Kings Highway
Rotated while businessmen in suits sipped

Beer and looked at themselves in the mirror.
Frat boys from the college would usually fight
In the parking lot, vomit on the cars.

WHEN NOTHING ELSE WAS OPEN

On Christmas and Easter, we'd go to Chinatown
To get dim sum and sponge cake, to look at shops
Where there really wasn't much we wanted.
Except, Toby liked cracker balls, the kind you
Throw to the sidewalk where they explode with
A faraway noise, not loud like a cherry bomb
Or even a firecracker, just a minor detonation.
It gave him pleasure to see how hard they'd hit
The pavement, right next to a lychee pit wedged
In a crack. The lychee pit ignored them, as did
The rest of us: me, his sister, the people walking
By. It was cold, and they—unlike us—had places
To get to. I'd look for a while at steamers and woks,
Cleavers, blue and white bowls, maybe a rice-cooker.
Next weekend, we could make Shanghai chicken wings.
I already had star anis and five-spice powder.
But the kids preferred Vietnamese noodles, even
Though I threatened getting a durian shake—cries of
"Dad, it smells like gasoline!" Then we'd laugh.
They had to be back to their mother's by seven.

Pennsylvania Avenue

Every day, the black SUVs sped
Down Pennsylvania Avenue
Carrying dignitaries, rulers,
Or generals, sometimes followed by
Truckloads of soldiers, automatic
Weapons held ready for an attack
That never happened. Across the street,
A large house owned by the Egyptian
Government, comings and goings at
Odd hours, an agency in charge of
Buying guns and planes — we never knew.

There were people who lived in Rock Creek
Park in tents and sleeping bags, watching
The traffic, drinking coffee, trying
To stay warm. Parts of the Pentagon
Were still blackened from 9/11,
And everyone remembered where they
Were when the plane hit. The husband of
A woman in my building had died
In the World Trade Center. Now, she was
Starting to date again. I saw her
In the elevator when I came
Home late from work. She was embarrassed.
The man who was with her had his arm
Around her waist. Tired, I just nodded,
Said good night, and got off at my floor.

One afternoon when I was at work,
My wife couldn't stop crying. She knocked
On the door of a doctor who lived
Across the hall, a kind woman
Who went with her to the hospital,
Returning that night with a bottle
Of antidepressants and a plan
To move quickly back to Florida.

D.C. had been hard. We had few friends.
My son was four and covered his ears
Walking down the sidewalk to shut out
The roar of traffic. In daycare, he
Wouldn't sit in the circle and sing
Good morning, but would wander around
The room looking for a window or,
Better yet, a door. He wanted to
Be somewhere else. The psychologist
Suggested a therapeutic school
In Maryland where kids wore helmets.
We decided to homeschool instead.

On weekends, we went to museums,
Took our dog for walks by the river.
In Miami, he'd chased squirrels and
Cats. Here, he flushed rats in the bushes.
In April, the cherry blossoms were
A white fire along the Potomac.

IN OUR STORIES

My son's in his room watching videos
And writing a novel about a bounty
Hunter in another galaxy who
Likes anime and can't be killed. Simon
And I share this house, meaning I wash the
Dishes, he helps out with the dog. Every
Night since he was six, we've gone for a walk,
Crafting stories together about elves
And trolls, warriors and thieves, and gods who
Don't care much what happens to people. A
Hundred generations of heroes and
Villains have been born and mostly met bad
Ends. The elves are still arrogant, greedy—
The trolls only marginally smarter
Than at the beginning. Simon asks each
Night about what's happened in the news. He
Doesn't like to read it for himself. I
Can't say I blame him. He's made a world where
Nothing much intrudes. He makes himself a
Pizza, some chocolate milk, plays indie
Video games I can't follow. Simon's
Four inches taller than I am, at least,
And his hair's grown halfway down his back. He
Doesn't go to work yet or drive a car,
And he's got no idea how to talk
With girls his age. He's worried that I'll die
Before he learns to take care of himself,
But he walks to the supermarket and
Buys parmesan cheese, pasta, tomato
Sauce, Oreos, and a half-gallon of
Milk—everything he needs. His mother and
I got divorced three years ago. In our
Stories, the gods play less and less a part.

"ARE YOU JEWISH?"

Three Lubavitcher kids stop me on
Lincoln Rd. "Are you Jewish," they ask.
I smile politely, keep moving and
Say, "Not now."
                    "You're Jewish all the time,"
One replies. Lubavitcher kids get
All the best lines.
                    I've never put on
Phylacteries in my life, and I
Don't go to *shul*, keep the sabbath, light
Candles, or turn down a Maine lobster.
Clearly, I'm not observant. I can
Say the quick version of the *kiddush*
Before the wine, the *motzi* over
Bread. Otherwise, I'm short on blessings.
I'm exactly the kind of bad Jew
The kids want to take to their Mitzvah-
Mobile and teach how to recite some
Prayers in Hebrew. Still, I don't think
That would make me Jewish. I'm too far
From the God I talk to when I shave,
The one who made the world so broken.

I read about a woman tortured
In Syria, an artist. I see
Her drawings of other women who
Were in prison with her and tortured
As she was. Her drawings have strong lines
And remind me of Kathe Kollwitz.
The pain doesn't radiate out as
Much as it collapses into the
Figure, a black hole strong enough to
Pull all the stars inside.

                    In Israel,
The rabbis say you're Jewish if your

Mother was Jewish, going all the
Way back to Eve, I guess. To me, it's
Different. You're Jewish if you look
For God in the world and can't find him,
If you look at portraits by a young
Woman who was tortured and you want
To go into a bathroom somewhere
And cry, if you know the angelic
Cavalry always arrives too late.

Next week, the Lubavitcher kids will
Stand at the same spot on Lincoln Rd.,
Blocking the sidewalk, believing that the
World will be redeemed and *Moshiac*
Will come if just one more bad Jew like
Me puts on phylacteries and prays.

Much as I'd like to join them, I won't.

FORTUNA

In a decade of backache and arthritic knees,
I find myself laughing like a sonofabitch,
Not yet senile but finding it all ridiculous.

Sometimes I stand at the bathroom sink and
Have one of those pretend conversations
With the Almighty. "I suppose this has been

For a reason," I say, not expecting an answer.
I have three children, two grandchildren,
And two former spouses. How many think

Of themselves as collateral damage? My
Friend Harold used to say in his nineties
That he'd been selfish—always done what he

Wanted, would take off on a motorcycle
To travel around Spain, go gambling on the
Weekends. Can't say I gamble, and I don't

Know anything about motorcycles—but I
Understand. *Mi compañera* would deny it,
Reassure me that I haven't been, but she

Doesn't realize how much I take from her,
Whether it's in bed touching or talking
Over coffee. "There aren't a lot of years left,"

She said, bringing her lips up to mine. I
Think too about my parents' lives, how badly
they ended, my mother's in dementia,

My father's in pain and confusion, sacrifices
To a god of bad outcomes, or perhaps to
Fortuna, ordained in Dante to shift the goods

Of the world from people to people, moving
In ecstasy while everyone curses her. There's
No reason to cancer or bad luck, and nobody's

Life has a happy ending. Boethius, in prison,
Preferred bad luck to good, despised Fortuna,
Her wheel, that Ostrogoth game show ending

In his execution. Did he get it right?
Tonight, it's raining so hard the roof shakes,
And I want to believe something outlasts us.

Poor, brilliant Boethius—I wish I had his
Certainty, thought mind or even reason
Endured, but I don't. They fall apart like the

Leather-bound books from my grandfather's
Library, spines turned to powder, peeling
Gold leaf, brown stains in the margins.

At the end, my mother weighed about sixty
Pounds. Her teeth fell out, and she couldn't
Form words. Her hands froze claw-like and curled

To her chest. She hadn't fed or wiped herself
For years. She had no visitors, but the nurses' aides
Left the television on, soap operas and Vanna

White hosting Wheel of Fortune. Boethius
Chose not to be a contestant but still lost. Did
Anyone win the Impala or the living room set?

Dante has already moved on to the next trench,
"A maggior pieta," to greater sorrow. You're right,
Mi amor. There aren't a lot of years left.

ELEGY

My Doberman never appeared sick until the morning
He couldn't get up from the kitchen floor. A long
Cancer had grown by his spine, and there wasn't much
I could do for him except tell the vet to end it.
He was lying on the metal table the same way
He'd been lying on the cold tiles of the floor at home.
Nothing was working. His eyes had the kind of confusion
I'd seen with my father when he was dying. Not like
In the movies, where characters die easily or in mid-sentence.
Oscar was eleven years old, which is old for that breed.
Big dogs don't live as long as little ones.
He liked to kill snakes by jumping in the air, landing
On top of one, then shaking it in his teeth till he broke something
And it would go limp. He chased squirrels he could never
Catch, and he was puzzled by the opossums who would go
Limp before he did anything. He'd just stand and look at them.
Now, the vet gave him an injection, and
He went limp, and I stood there almost as puzzled
As he'd been by the opossums. About a week later,
They sent me his ashes in a box.

ELSEWHERE

A fortuneteller told me once I'd
Never be satisfied. He was right,
But he didn't say why and couldn't
Have known how I'd stood by the window
At night, watching cars pass on the street,
Their red taillights receding into
Other lives, parties, restaurants, love
Affairs, a woman who would place her
Hand on my neck, move our lips closer
Until they touched and opened. There were
Highways that cut across my city,
Leading to bigger cities, ones with
Bookstores, with cafés, movie theaters
That showed seven films at the same time,
Concerts that filled stadiums. How hard
Was it to guess I wanted things I
Hadn't even imagined? Last night,
We sat in a café together,
Drinking Cuban coffee, strings of white
Lightbulbs surrounding us as we talked.
Could that fortuneteller fifty
Years ago in an East Texas town
Have predicted this: how the air pressed
Cool against my skin, how soft your hand
Felt when we walked down to the bay, saw
The lights of cars crossing the causeway?
At the end of the street, two men were
Night fishing, casting lures over dark
Water, then reeling them quickly back
To shore. What did they make of us, this
Man and woman no longer young but
With undiminished desire, moved by
Those faint lights from the causeway, by planes
On their way somewhere else, and streetlamps
Reflecting in shallow pools the same
Color as the sky? Above us loomed the

Sharp-angled ramps and concrete tiers of
Parking garages and some massive
New buildings where no one seemed to live.
On the street, oak trees overturned the
Pavement, and scrawny cats stalked ducks who'd
Gathered by a fence. Wherever we
Live is temporary, foreign. Our
Lips touch. We take shelter where we can.

Miami Beach Prepares for Climate Change

I don't know what a city is supposed to resemble
Anymore. This one is just a collection of buildings
Sticking their fists up at the sky, architectural
Anger reflecting the sunlight or lit up at night in
Neon colors, electric blue, magenta, mouthwash green.
My friend Frank once had an apartment here that faced
The water. Each morning, the sun burned through his window,
And he'd stand on his balcony with a cup of coffee or
Tea and watch the early sunbathers or the birds diving for fish.
Sometimes at dawn, he'd see a cruise ship elbow its way
Into the channel to dock before the passengers were awake.
The parking garage underneath his building
Used to flood every time there was bad weather.
Cars that weren't moved in time were destroyed by saltwater,
Smells of leaking oil and mold. I had an office a few
Blocks away, and we'd meet for lunch
At one of the restaurants where you could sit outside,
Eat sandwiches, and talk. What would we say to each other now,
Sitting over French pastries at a table on Lincoln Road?
Even with repairs, the streets here still flood when the tide's
Too high, the Atlantic curls and breaks on the other side
Of the seawall, and the lost cigarette lighter in the sand is washed
Toward Europe or Africa. The black outlines of cargo ships
Still move east, then north—not like ships at all, just cardboard
Boxes painted and set adrift—and tourists in rented sports cars
Still drive back and forth, looking for a place to park.
What can I say, Frank? Not much has changed.

Running Late

Traffic slows for no obvious reason.
The front ends replicate faces, lights for
Eyes, chrome grills for mouths, teeth, metal versions
Of ourselves, exhaust pipes in back, gas tanks
Like our own desire, invisible as
Possible. Through the rolled-up windows, we
See each other, eyes on road or distance
Or glancing down to turn up the music,
Disembodied voices. We are minds on
Parallel trajectories, fantasies
Of trading one body for another.
Yogis could do that in old folktales, send
Their minds to the next village, to possess
A rich merchant with a beautiful wife.
(The yogis in those tales are not saintly.)
Even when we're on time, we're running late,
Unsure where we're supposed to be or when
We're supposed to be there. Billboards try to
Sell us jewelry, air conditioning—
Implied threat: "Your Wife Is Hot!" If you don't
Buy a new AC, a yogi from the
Next village might take over your body.
Who isn't late for something? I had a
Friend, an observant Jew, who left his car
By the side of the road at sunset and
Walked the rest of the way home. Perhaps, it's
Better to be late. A year afterwards,
He died of an aneurysm. Now he's
Just memory, flimsy as cellophane
Or radio waves floating unseen in
The air. We imagine our dead pulling
Over, closing the doors of their bodies
And walking away, a slice of pizza
Unfinished, a napkin left unfolded.
Somedays, there's nothing on the radio.

HIDING

Under the bed is a good place. Outside
In the bushes, it's too hot, and there're bugs.

Behind the coat rack in the closet it's
Cool and dark. The jackets smell of the dry

Cleaners. Often, the plastic covering
Is still on. You can sit on the floor and

Listen to the noise the walls make, the fan
On the air conditioner. But, the best

Part about hiding is the voices you
Can barely hear, sometimes irritated,

Sometimes joking, sometimes you can't tell which.
From under the door, a crack of light makes

The plastic covers shiny. Children aren't
Supposed to pull them down over their heads,

But they make your face weird in the mirror.
When do you think they're going to find you?

In Retrospect

Today, I think it's the world that's real, not me.
I close my eyes and listen to traffic, a dog's nails
Scratching at the pavement, someone's radio,

And voices speaking a language I don't recognize—
It sounds a little like French but not much. There's
Something I don't like about the poems I'm reading.

The paper is rough against my fingers, or
Maybe it's the coffee or the people walking by.
It's too easy to imagine it all the same, but with

Me airbrushed out of the picture. The street would
Be just as crowded. The taqueria on the other side
Would be just as busy. At the next table, there's a kid

In high school meeting with an advisor to discuss
Plans for college. She is exuberant about his options.
Her sister went to Tulane. She is from California,

But doesn't say how she ended up here, why she's
Sitting in that café chair, talking about universities,
Careers. The poems I'm reading are hopeless. They're

The poems of a man who's dug himself a hole and
Can't climb out. Women have betrayed him, and friends
Are otherwise occupied—the poems are performances

Of all the things he can't make happen. It makes me
Sleepy, and I skip ahead in the book. I do that a lot,
See what's going to happen, then work backwards. It

All makes sense then. Every story goes wrong somewhere,
And this way you can see it, how who he was slid off
The table and cracked against the concrete floor. It

Could happen to anyone, myself included. Maybe it
Already has, and I don't know it. This morning, I read
Text messages from a cancer patient to her boss. She

Described how after the surgery the wound wouldn't
Stop draining, how uncertain she was if she was really
Getting better. She wanted to believe the drugs were

Working and that her doctors could keep her alive. I
Don't know what happened to her, but nothing seemed
To be going right. She switched hospitals, doctors,

Medications. Skipping ahead in her story doesn't help.
Sometimes, there aren't any right choices. Endings
Are always arbitrary or banal or both. But, I don't

Get up and leave. I'm meeting my son in a few
Minutes. He's twenty and unconcerned with endings.
Later, I get a call from a friend in Los Angeles. When he

Left the hospital, his sister had thrown away all
His books, his notes, photographs. He's starting again now
With nothing, inhaling who he wants to be next, the

Future like some odd smell you can't identify. If
This "I" weren't here, would it make any difference? The
Question is nonsensical. I was never here to begin with.

III.

"A fairer House than Prose"

"A fairer House than Prose"

Maybe the now-extinct dodo bird will flap
Its useless wings in the glass case
Of the natural history museum.

Maybe highways will roll up like yoga mats
Until they crumble beneath their own weight,
Spilling asphalt, cars, gas stations, and rest stops
Onto an endless prairie.

Maybe I'll open the mailbox today and
Find Dante's Paradiso wrapped inside
Itself, a red enfolded rose.

Maybe someone's heart will literally
Break, a ventricle cracking from sorrow
And desire never manifest.

Maybe there'll be a knock at the door
And on the doorstep a burning bush, a voice
Calling me by a name I don't recognize.

Maybe I'll get in line at the movie theater
Down the street and see dead philosophers
Approaching the ticket window.

Maybe they'll holler to me, "Hey,
We're saving you a seat!"

LUNCH WITH KAFKA

I'm fixing a sandwich in the kitchen when he comes in,
Dark hair, skinny, already coughing.
His English isn't so good, and I don't speak German
Or Yiddish, but that doesn't seem to matter.
Because I'm just starting to put mustard on two slices
Of whole wheat bread, I gesture to it with my head,
Sort of a sideways nod, and he smiles and shakes his
Head up and down, universal sign for "Yes, please."
All I have is sliced turkey and cheese, but
Dead people aren't picky eaters. I get out two
Plates and put a sandwich on each. He helps me
Carry them to the table. There's so much I want to ask,
But I don't think he's here to answer questions. The
First time I try—*Why did you want all those stories*
Burned?—he just looks at me and shrugs. Maybe
He didn't understand, or maybe he means he doesn't know,
Or maybe the answer is too complicated. I try again,
Franz, did you see it all coming: the war, the burning cities,
The Nazis? This time, he looks serious, but
He still doesn't speak. Instead, he gets up from the
Table and walks to the kitchen to boil some water.
I watch him make us both tea. How does he know where
Everything is, the cups, the teapot, even the sugar?
Then, he brings it all back and pours a cup for me and
One for him. His hands warm themselves against the
Porcelain. His shoulders drop down a little as he sits,
His elbows just off the table, and I get the message.
There's not much we can do for each other. Do
Whatever you can.

KNOSSOS

The turning passages wrap round themselves,
Intestines of adolescent girls and boys,
Skulls broken, arms twisted askew or off.
All the time, Theseus dreams of a bronze sword
Cutting the fetid air, a spool of white
Thread that unwinds as he walks, the breathing of
A creature that didn't ask for birth or death,
That never wanted to be part of a story.
The labyrinth does not contain Theseus or
The beast he'll kill. The labyrinth coils tight
Inside them both. It's growing late, though who
Could tell that in the skyless dark? The Minotaur
Feels sleepy, flesh-drunk. The horns on his head
Bend toward the ground. Theseus will not come
Tonight. He is still a dream, another passage,
One that turns when it appears to go straight, that ends
At a blank wall where bull and man collide,
Look up, and recognize each other, familiar
As the face in the bathroom mirror, the screen
Of the television when it darkens, or the glass
Frame on the photograph above your desk.
If the Minotaur cries out, the cry is sharp-
Pitched and sudden. Tomorrow, the philosophers
Will gather near the marketplace. Presidents
And cabinet ministers will settle their differences
Over chilled wine and platters of shrimp curled
Like small fingers. Tank commanders will give
The order to fire. Tomorrow, the philosophers
Will teach the principles of government:
How much grain should be distributed, what day
Of the month unemployment checks should go out,
Whether prostitutes should pay taxes.
In the labyrinth, the Minotaur is either asleep
Or dead. It's too dark to see which. Theseus
Is on a ship headed back to Athens, his black
Sail engorged with wind, his thread abandoned,

Trailing like a vein or artery toward
A dry, broken heart at the earth's center.
Far away, Daedalus stands on a hilltop, weeping.
Far away, Icarus crashes into the sea.

THE SLEEP OF REASON

For Jose Armando Garcia

Reason falls asleep, an exhausted child,
The youngest of memory's darlings, head
Resting in the crook of an arm—how

Eighteenth century, how age of the guillotine,
How literate! His dreams, will-of-the-wisps
With teeth and claws, with jagged beaks

Pointed as those white hats inquisitors
Placed on their victims, the ones
Who would know fire like Giordano Bruno

Or the rack like Machiavelli. Poor reason,
So blameless for all this, condemned to
Read Dostoevsky until he understands what

It means to burn money. Poor reason, who
Can't help but fall asleep, waiting so long
For Saturn to devour his children.

I.B. SINGER'S BUILDING

Back then, I used to live around the corner
From I.B. Singer. He was really two, maybe
Three, blocks away, but memory makes us
Next-door neighbors. The West Side was still rough
Around the edges, the developers just
Starting to move in. Nice stores had opened
On Broadway, but when I walked my dog at night,
The sidewalk was lined with hookers waiting
For a car to pull up at the curb. They'd ask
About the dog. He was a black chow with
A purple tongue and not particularly
Friendly, but if you're standing there in six-inch
Heels for hours, he'd probably take your mind
Off how much your feet hurt. Columbus Ave.
Hadn't been gentrified either. There was a
Bar where the fights would spill into the street.
Once, I had to duck behind a car because
Somebody was shooting. There were none of
The cafeterias Singer wrote about,
But there were still people who spoke Yiddish
And spent their savings to go to concerts at
Lincoln Center or buy a chocolate babka
From the bakery. On 72nd, there was
A dairy restaurant where Singer, who was
A vegetarian, might have eaten, though
For good dairy you had to go downtown.
Now, the waitresses who worked there, who dressed
In pink and white uniforms, are dead, like most
Of their customers. The young moved to Brooklyn
And the old to nursing homes. My dog died a
Few years later, and for a while, I taught at
Fordham, where some of my students were
Characters in Singer's stories, an actress
From the Yiddish theater who'd studied with
Stanislavski, a professor who'd lived through
A pogrom during the Pilsudski Republic,

A Lubavitcher who'd left to become a
Lesbian and smuggle bibles into the
USSR. The older ones talked about
Hungarian modernists or could recite
From Mickiewicz. It was what they'd brought with
With them from Europe, what they didn't lose.
Back then, Singer lived in a pre-war building
At 86th and Broadway. I lived across
From the middle school, in a tenement on
85th between Columbus and Amsterdam.
School kids smoked pot in the entranceway, and
The super was a drunk who lived in a shack on
The roof. On Christmas morning, he banged
On all the doors, crying because no one had
Given him a present. I don't think things like
That happened in I.B. Singer's building.

BAUDELAIRE

He doesn't look much like a hero—
Limp bowtie of a dandy, *flaneur*,
Fallen to the next class down below
Where he began, imploring mother

For a bit more allowance. But to
Himself, he's the latest in a line
Of poets, a white marble statue
Crowned with leafless laurel—a bad sign—

Pissed on at night by vagrants who wag
Sore pricks, by day, dogs that lift a leg

Saluting the rich who drink better
Wine and whose mistresses display
Upon the stage pink flesh that debtors
Can't afford. He dines in a café

To save money, asks for a carafe
Of water, announcing to a friend
It's doctor's orders. At nine he's off
To visit Jeanne, but he's not let in.

She has other guests who can afford
Gifts he can't. She tells him she's grown bored.

Outside, the carriages, crowds sweep by,
The evening stars invisible where
He walks. Only lights from the city
Decorate sky, the rooftops, the air.

Exhausted, finally he retreats,
His collar damp with sweat, the room chilled.
He's borrowed money from men he hates.
He could write a review but feels ill.

No, a poem… and Jeanne a vampire.
He imagines breasts, her thick black hair….

Samuel Beckett Gives André the Giant a Ride to School

From everything I've read, this really happened.
They were neighbors in France, and Beckett had a car.
Beyond that, we don't know much. Imagine the young André
Squeezing himself into a tiny Citroën 2CV, his head sticking out
Through the rolled-up roof. Imagine Beckett asking
André about his classes, what he was reading, whether his classmates
Made his life more difficult. Or perhaps, it wasn't anything like that.
Perhaps, Beckett and André were both quiet on those rides. I doubt
André followed theater or had read *Waiting for Godot*, and because
Beckett gave him a ride, he didn't have to wait for anyone.
As for Beckett, he would just have enjoyed not having to be himself.
Yes, I think it's likely they were quiet.

CARAVAGGIO

Caravaggio seems to have understood how
Hard it is to cut off a man's head, how the blood
Shoots disconcertingly from severed arteries.
His Judith is a novice to the work of killing. Her
Brow is furrowed with the new concentration
Required, without sense of future or past, just
Holofernes's surprise and bulging eyes,
His mouth wide open as though he is
Trying to swallow his own death. But her grip
On his hair does not relax, and the sword stays
Heavy in her right hand. The job is only half-way
Done. A few locks of reddish hair brush against her
Ear, mirroring subtly the curl of her lips. She
Wears a pearl earring tied with a black ribbon. There
Was a message in that ribbon, but her would-be
Lover failed to notice. They say her white blouse was
A late addition, that once, she was naked from
The waist up, just as Holofernes is naked, his hand
Still pressed against the folds of the blanket.
To the side, an old woman glares at the dying
General and holds a cloth bag to catch the head.

CRIVELLI'S MADONNA AND CHILD

The world is just as beautiful as it's hurt.
A fly's landed next to the child, the stone is cracked.
Poised on a cushion and yellow cloth, alert,
Bird clutched to heart, he observes but doesn't act.

A fly's landed next to the child, the stone is cracked,
A knobby gourd, ripe apples shade the skies.
Bird clutched to heart, he observes but doesn't act.
The world is broken marble; we are flies.

A knobby gourd, ripe apples shade the skies,
Mauve silk and branches held by nothing seen.
The world is broken marble; we are flies.
Behind him is the orchard's endless green.

Mauve silk and branches held by nothing seen,
Poised on a cushion and yellow cloth, alert,
Behind him is the orchard's endless green.
The world is just as beautiful as it's hurt.

DANSE MACABRE

When you write the word *death,* nothing happens.
No one dies. The sky doesn't darken.
A fountain pen hovers above a notebook. The nib
Touches the paper. It leaves a blue spot where
The page begins. The spot becomes a word and the
Word a sentence. The notebook yawns in its
Leather case. Your dry hand strokes the page and tells
It to behave, brushes away crumbs of brioche,
Dabs at a red spot of jam, awkwardly touches the pink
Stain. Each time the pen speaks, the paper replies.
A stray dog crawls closer to one of the tables.
A cloud hangs like an awning over the afternoon,
The noise of traffic, a mathematical equation.
When there are too many letters, the words clump
Together, automobile exhaust hangs in the air.
You find it hard to breathe.

When you write the word *death,* no one cares.
You're not writing anyone's death in particular.
You're not the governor at a polished oak desk,
Signing a death warrant, then checking his watch.
When you write the word *death,* you imagine
A hedge of roses, large thorns, twisted stems and
Blooms, splashing white, red, and pink into
Your eyes. They burn for a moment at the thought.
You turn your face toward the black soil and the
Roots. You think *finally* you've arrived at something,
But the soil is full of seedlings, purposeful insects,
The droppings of a cat.

                    When you write the word
Death, you think it's a sacrament. You hold it
On your tongue. The page has wrapped itself into
A church spire, the arches of a cathedral, pews
Filled with worshippers. When did you last sit in
Such a place? Old women lighting candles, frowning

Saints—they all would stare at you, know that you
Don't belong. So, you write *death* a little off to
The side, almost at the margin, the fountain pen
Moving too slowly on the page, the letters turning
Thick the way a child would write or an invalid,
Falling asleep in a chair.

                    Perhaps, you are beginning
What will be a fairy tale. *Death* is a princess locked
In a tower. The pen curls like the tail of a dragon or
Steam from a teapot. In the story, *death* will have its
Portrait painted by a great artist. It will wear robes made
Of fur and velvet, and its hands will be extraordinarily
White, its fingers narrow. The artist will put much effort
Into the lips and eyes, the forehead that wrinkles a
Little with all that it's observed. The thought gives
You confidence. You touch the pen once more to the page,
Writing *death* over and over again. But, no matter
How many times you write it, nothing happens.

A Friend Writes

For Maria Gogni & Alejandro M. Drewes

A friend writes it's raining in Buenos Aires.
Sky and street are the same color. Windows
Are blurred, fogged at the edges, and the soft
Figures of children in yellow raincoats float
Leaf-like along the pavement. No one
Sits outside in the cafés. Even the mannequins
In evening gowns and high heels frown
As water pools outside the thick glass
That separates them from the sidewalk and
Traffic. If it rained for forty days, what
Would you save on your ark? What books would
You take with you? What paintings would you
Keep dry? Would you arrange memories of
Your city with their spines neatly shelved in
Alphabetical order? Would you remember
Monuments in the cemetery, a bar where you
And Alejandro ordered carafes of young
Wine, where the waiters always smiled at you
Then returned to cigarettes, arguments over
Football? And the poems, which would you
Rescue: Pizarnik, Paz, Rilke, Borges, Paul Celan?
Which would you read aloud as waves slap
Against the wooden hull and rain splatters on the
Deck above your head? From a window on
The top floor of the library, someone is
Looking down at the cars and water, buses and
Trucks, at the brown wake splashing behind them.
Streetlamps glow in pale afternoon light.

NOTRE-DAME DE PARIS

April 15, 2019

On the screen, images of Notre Dame
Burning, the spire falling slowly into the nave—
Water from firehoses unable to reach high
Enough to save it. Tonight, it's still smoking,
A black ruin in the center of Paris. I was
Eighteen when I first saw it. It was night,
And I'd just arrived. I was staying in a
Room with big windows on the Left Bank,
And I went for a long walk along the Seine,
Looking up at gargoyles in the dark,
Staring at gray stone, carved blocks that
Might as well have been time itself, heavy,
Immobile—our lives passing in front of
Them unnoticed, the way our parents'
Lives passed, our DNA strings
A cliché compared to blocks of stone and
Arches. I don't know whether I believed in God—
I wavered then—but I believed in time.
I had grown up with old oak trees, too large
To embrace, with pecan and pine older
Than the houses in my neighborhood.
They seemed indestructible, though I knew
They weren't. These stone walls and parapets
Were older than the trees I remembered, and
The Seine that night was the same color
As the sky, darker than black. If you'd
Told me it was polished by giant hands, I
Might have believed you. The stars seemed
To break apart against the surface. Now,
The cathedral is darker than the water that
Surrounds it. Blackness of burnt wood and
Scarred stone, of wet soot and ash. It should be
Daylight soon on the Île de la Cité.
People walking to work will detour to look
From upstream or down, not quite believing
What they see.

While I Slept

While I was asleep, a flock of geese landed in the tree by the fence,
The one with high branches that look down on the houses and golf course.

When I was asleep, a flock of geese landed on the roof and on the fence.
They called to each other, anxious and hungry, looking for red
    earthworms, black beetles.

When I was asleep, a flock of geese landed and flew off again.
They weren't done traveling, and there was nothing here worth their time.

Somewhere to the south, there are marshes and islands, horizons of
    sand and water.
Somewhere to the south, it never gets cold and there's plenty to eat.

When I was asleep, a flock of geese stopped for a moment, then kept going.

IV.

The Winter Ducks

THE WINTER DUCKS

For Ximena Gómez

I love it that they are not like us,
More like artists and writers from a
Hundred years ago, inhabiting
Cafés in Warsaw or Paris, chairs
Crowding together, pecking at each
Other, and having affairs. Preening
White feathers, they roost beneath an old
Hong Kong Orchid, the red kind with blooms
That are almost purple. They prefer
Manet's "Le Déjeuner sur l'herbe" to
The rigors of cubism, and when
They argue, one or two will get up
And glide elegantly to the far
Side of the pond, wings reflecting
Mottled sunlight patterning the brown
Water. Tomorrow, I'll bring some bread.

ACROSS FROM THE OPERA

It's been raining, off and on, all day, the sky
Shifting sets: Scene 2, a sunny afternoon, the
King of Naples is traveling by ship, Scene 3,

Clouds move in quickly, stage left, cue
Lightning and thunder, sailors rush onstage,
Distraught as sparrows, their wings too wet to fly.

If I were sitting by a window in a café
Somewhere in Italy, I'd order coffee and
Biscotti with pistachios or almonds,

And watch the fine mist gather on tables
Stacked outside and open a book, maybe poems,
Maybe science fiction or a crime novel.

When I look up, the sky will either have cleared
Or grown darker. Scene 4, evening, the shops
Lit with a yellow glow. Women pass wearing

Scarves, stepping carefully over the puddles.
Mannequins stare out at them, shamelessly.
I close the book, pay my check, exit.

CAFFÈ CORRETTO

Wet cold from the Adriatic, the
Dolomites' jagged shadows on the
Horizon. On the dock, I can smell
Salt water and rust, hear the creaking
Of brine-soaked wood when the waves shove at
The pilings. Earlier, there might have
Been fog thick enough to make islands
Disappear. But, I wasn't awake.
A baker's left rolls by the locked door
Of a café. The owner opens
Quickly and takes them inside. When he
Turns the sign around, I walk in and
Stand at the counter, ordering a
Caffè corretto, espresso mixed
With grappa. The warmth starts at my belt,
Then it moves out toward my hands, feet.
Carts pass outside, picking up garbage.
The sounds of the market grow louder.
I stop and remind myself that this
Isn't real. It's a memory from
Years ago, still bright as an orange
Raincoat displayed in a shop window,
Or morning sunlight reflected on
A kitchen table. I love this place,
But maybe I love it because I
Don't live here, because it's not where I
Work, because I imagine my life
Floating on top of it like a hat
Somebody's lost in the water, caught
By a current before it could be
Retrieved. Underneath a stone archway,
An art gallery sells glass sculptures,
Paintings with blobs of red and yellow,
Posters from last year's exhibitions.
If this were real, I'd stop and look. I'd
Browse in some store that sold wool sweaters,
Elegant ties, or that suede jacket

I've always wanted. Just out of reach,
The lost hat floats down a canal, caught
In the stream, pushed one way, another,
But always moving away from where
I'd planned to go. For an instant, the
Wind moves it toward me. I reach out, grab.

SCRITCH-SCRATCH

Dogs don't use words. They look up or
Scratch at the door to go out, make
Whining noises or bark. But words
Aren't dogs, like dogs aren't avocados,
Cracks in the pavement, or lines
For hopscotch.

            The first world was
Without words. Just pushing from inside,
Empty stomach, dry tongue, sex—the rain
Soaking everything, hoof-prints, deer droppings
By a green bush, unripe berries. In the second
World, words were scritch-scratch for apples
And meat, for tigers and waterholes, for
Rivers and fire, the thing that wasn't
In front of you, thing wanted, thing that
Shouldn't be forgotten. Then, the time
When words made up their own world,
When there were words for other
Words, a whole world that couldn't be seen,
Everything invisible, everything possible,
Not just tiger, but the god of tigers, the
Moon who mated with the ocean and
The sun who died beneath the waves and
Was always reborn. Everything turned
Scritch-scratch. The baby's first word, the
Words of the dying.

            Left behind in
The world of things were apples and dirt,
Cows and sidewalks, tree limbs stretching
Above the avenues, musicians playing for
Coins from passersby. Words claimed
The limits of the world, and what was
Beyond was only the white border of
A map, empty of everything but fingerprints.

In the beginning, they said, were words,
Existing before things, before rain, sunlight,
Before creatures crawled out of the sea, before
First roots and grass-blades, first stars
Rising and setting. In the beginning, they
Said, was scritch-scratch, because the world
That's not here doesn't die and isn't born. And
The dirt and the apples, the dogs and avocados,
Even the waterfalls, sharp rocks, were just
Accidents, shadows in a cave at night,
Firelight or flashlight making scritch-
Scratch on the walls. Rivers were no longer
Wet, fish no longer slippery. Rivers were
Lines on a map made from words—the
Ocean waves: instances; the starlight: energy.
People wore shoes so as not to feel the earth.

Only the stubborn refused the salvation of
Words—exiled from the city of
Ideas, of God, they praised the world they
Saw, tasted, and did so blasphemously,
In words. They praised the cold stink of
Corpses, the clean smell of rain in summer,
The uselessness of love, all things forgotten,
The pain the bricks feel under the weight
Of mortar and wood, of other bricks, memories
Of wet clay and air. They praised their
Bodies, which were nothing like the idea
Of bodies, strong and perfect. They praised
The paunch of their stomachs and the weakness
Of their legs and shoulders, and they praised
The bodies they loved, changing as they changed,
Which unlike words would not last forever,
Preferred the fragile texture of living skin to
Scritch-scratch on stone. They were stubborn,
And the words loved them for their stubbornness.

Reverie

Inside a dream, there's no description,
No painter with bright oils and canvas

Surveying a shoreline of mangroves
And mosquitoes. There's no one to whom

The dream happens. The face that stares back
From the mirror has not been born. If

There's a beach here, no one's ever stretched
Naked on its sand, listening to

Sea birds shout at each other, flash white
Feathers between one wave and the next.

The clock has yet to be invented.
Men point at the sun, try to think of

Words for how the world happens: the black
Wind that moves across the sunset sky

When fire meets water and air turns cold.
At such times, is the mind dry or wet?

No pair of eyes regards the tilted
Palms or shuts their lids against the glare.

A dog squats, shits in the parking lot.
The dream exists but not the dreamer.

OCTOBER

In October, each sunburnt blue sky
Worries us. The high pressure before
A hurricane looks like this, a wind
Out of the east or south, dust carried
All the way from the Sahara on
Heat-driven currents, rows of broken
White clouds pushed toward this distant side of
The world. I think how much dust I've breathed
In sixty-five years, how the Gobi,
The Kalahari, even the ten
Deserts of Australia, have all swirled
In my lungs, mixed with auto exhaust,
With the dry air conditioning of
Hospitals and office buildings, damp
Mists of Venetian canals before
Sunrise, the marshes on the North Shore
Of Massachusetts, the smoke from fires
In the Everglades—I don't have to
Travel anywhere to see what floats
In my blood. In India, they pour
Oil on a corpse, light it, and watch as
The ash drifts up into the sky. In
Miami, I take a quiet breath.

NEW YEAR'S DAY
For Sean Thomas Dougherty

This year there were no parties. Our friends
Were sick with flu or busy caring
For family sick with flu, but we'd
Still stayed up late talking and drinking
Prosecco, the remains of dinner,
Arroz con pollo, left on our plates.
The next day, we planned to assemble
Ikea furniture, a desk and
Chair. I confess, the chair is still in
Pieces. Instead, we cooked black-eyed peas
And cornbread, which made me think of my
Friend Frank who died just a year ago
Because I'd always bring him black-eyed
Peas on New Year's. Then, we read poems
From websites or posted on Facebook.
Sean's poem about the editor
Who sent him a rejection on New
Year's morning was particularly
Good. It made me think about the things
We decide should give us hope, this day
Chosen arbitrarily by some
Roman emperor or pope to be
The beginning of—what?—not the end
Of autumn or middle of winter.
Random as the throw of dice on an
Italian afternoon, a man looks
Up from his writing and says, "Yes, I'll
Begin it here, not at solstice or
Equinox—the sun shall receive no
Primacy." In January, the
Sky thickens with clouds thrown like pillows
Across an unmade bed. Where Sean lives,
Snow's inevitable, but here in
Florida, winter is the good time,
Nights mild and cloudless, Orion and

The Pleiades visible as soon
As it's dark, almost as bright as the
Fireworks we watched at midnight, showers
Of red and gold, falling on rooftops
And fences, bell curves of trees, unknown
Yards, and streets where the cars slow to stare.
So, for no reason at all, we cook
A special meal, open the wine we've
Been saving, sip espresso sweetened
With Kahlua and turn the pages
Inside of us, mumbling once again
Words we hope will grant wishes, protect
From harm. A new year begins today.

RECIPES

These are the recipes for dishes
We never cooked, the rice pilafs that

Always looked delicious in the book's
Color photos, the green herbs laid out

On a white plate, the golden piles of
Cumin and turmeric, the cakes soaked

In sugar syrup and flavored with
Anis. These are the memories of

Dinners we've never eaten, roast ducks
With cracking, brittle skin the color

Of dark tea, loaves of braided challah
Punctuated with raisins, French beans

With butter and almonds. These are the
Bite-sized regrets we've served each other,

Then forgotten, the phone calls we wish
We'd made, apologies left on the

Kitchen counter—to dry, wrinkle, rot.

WITHOUT EXPLANATION

Today the house was filled with dying bees.
I don't know where they came from, maybe the

Air conditioning, but they hummed furiously,
Banging at the sliding-glass door, blinded by

Afternoon sun, some of them trapped between
One pane and another. I tried sweeping them

Out with the green broom I keep in the closet.
I tried putting out a bowl of sugared water

As well—but the bees kept piling up on the floor
Or floated helpless in the sugared water.

Later, making dinner, I could still hear them,
That small cacophony of confusion, defeat,

As their delicate wings smashed hopelessly
Against the overhead lights in the kitchen.

"Of Almost Savage Torpor"

For Francisco Larios

It's July, but the pink trumpet tree
In the neighbor's yard still has blossoms.
I stand up from reading email and

Stare at the back fence, its wooden slats
Bleached by afternoon sun. Politics
Has become real for us lately, but

We're not able to change much. When
Wordsworth heard Napoleon had been
Crowned by the Pope, he compared it to

"A dog returning to its vomit."
Ortega and Murillo and their
First cousin in Venezuela, still scratch

The ears of German Shepherds as they
Order beatings, deaths, have their photos
Taken with bishops. It would have been

The same two hundred years ago, but
With oils and canvas and more gold braid.
My friend, Francisco, has started a

Journal. He tells me revolutions
Only look like they happen all at
Once. For years countries wobble, small acts

Accumulating, deals going on
That no one talks about. Then, the doors
Of the Bastille splinter open, and

Everything seems to have changed in an
Instant. I want to believe him, but
The quiet scares me. The world exhaled

Months ago. The business of staying
Alive resumed, finding food, clothes, a
Place to live. Refugees settled in,

Anxiously applying for visas,
Knowing too much about what's going
On and too little. I feel the same way

About my own country. I can't make
Sense out of mobs chanting, "Send her back"
Or the people who encourage them.

I feel like it should be night outside
With rain running down the sides of the
House, but it's 3:00 p.m. The sky is

Relentlessly blue, oblivious.

Pieter Bruegel the Elder Looks at Two Monkeys

The monkeys know better than to move.
They squat in the window with rounded

Backs, one stares, ignoring the painter.
The other's face turns down and away.

Iron clamps by their hips attach to
Chains. If they climbed African tree limbs

Once, they don't remember. The river
Behind them is brown and busy with

Commerce, ships coming and going like
Birds diving through mist. In the distance

Antwerp spreads its sea-green towers. The
Monkeys don't appreciate the view.

Auden tells us the old masters were
Never wrong about suffering, how

The world goes about its business and
Ignores torture, murder of children.

The monkeys know this instinctively.
They have not been tied to the rack or

Their small teeth extracted with pliers.
On the hierarchy of crimes, their chains

Do not merit notice. In return,
They refuse to acknowledge Antwerp

With its towers, ships, and swooping birds.
They will not even acknowledge the

Painter who draws their delicate black
Hands and feet, the rich grain of their fur.

The painter's hand moves as he sketches,
But the monkeys refuse to notice.

PRIVATE THINGS

For Ken Johnson

We sat over lunch: chicken Marbella and
Potatoes, a dark red wine from Sonoma, then
Espresso and panettone— my perfect meal.
We spoke about our days, classes we'd
Taught in prison, funny stories about mistakes
We'd made. This is what friends do. They have
Another slice of bread, a little cheese, and
Remember things, translations of poems, false
Cognates (more laughter). You said that
After you'd read the book Ximena translated
You knew me better. I laughed again, but
Really almost blushed. This is what I never took
Into account. The words on the page add up
To something, a voice that's different from how I wish
I sounded, embarrassed now that my troubles have
Been so small, that my hurts healed so quickly—
Embarrassed also to have spoken about so many
Private things, what love feels like when you're
Too old to take it for granted and too young to
Be able to understand it. Maybe, I never
Will understand the way air pours out of my lungs
In those moments, the way the room vanishes.
My parents used to say there are things gentlemen
Don't talk about. But, what can you do
When it's too late to be a gentleman?

THE SYLLABUS

It's the day before the start of classes, and
I'm trying to think of a poem to give my students

Tomorrow. Something to help them get started,
Maybe by Jack Gilbert or Sean Thomas

Dougherty. I thumb through the pages of some
Books and think again about how our poems

Contain us, become the balance sheets that
Add up our lives. How hopeless we are. How

Our desire to be heard betrays us. My students
Won't know anything about that yet. For them,

There's just the satisfaction of getting it said, of
Taking what they see, what's caused them pain,

And turning it to paper and ink, and I encourage them,
Applaud successes. It's the only way they'll climb

Over the razor wire and race across the night sky like
Satan in Paradise Lost. Of course, they wouldn't

Like that comparison. Most are believers. But,
Tell me there's nothing Satanic about this need

To be heard, this lump in the chest—maybe I
Should compare it to the creatures in Aliens who

Burst through the stomachs of unfortunate astronauts.
My students might approve of that one. There's

Something soiled about this business of poetry. It has
To be OK not to be polite, to use words like "mucus"

Or "bloodstain" or "motel room," to remember the
Times you hurt someone without meaning to—but you

Did nonetheless. Poems are all about "nonetheless,"
The way what happened can't be changed, a child's

Fever, the smell of sweat on blankets and sheets,
Women who shook their heads and walked the other

Way, days when the sidewalk's cold pushed through
The rubber soles of your sneakers, sharp and wet as

The teeth of those creatures in Aliens. Nonetheless,
There is something to say, something that's clean and

Pure as a haiku by Basho, the smell of pine tree bark
Sticky with resin, the blue of ocean when the sun

Opens a door in the waves. This time of year, it rains
Every day. Outside the prison, the water level

In the Everglades rises. Birds move to the trees or
Rest on the fence. Our poems will always tell the stories

We'd rather not hear, how much a cup of coffee might
Mean to you if you couldn't afford it. There's a guard

Who leaves her travel-mug unattended sometimes.
Someone might take a long sip and move away quickly.

Poems are also about stealing, days or minutes we
Hide somewhere back of that gray mass of

Brain and fluid behind our eyes, time we don't
Want to lose, glimpses of blue feathers nesting

In the marshes, dark brown water getting
Higher and higher. I can't afford to ask if writing

Poems matters, to them or to me. Rain sputters against
The roof, pooling deep and black in the parking lot.

I decide on Larry Levis's "Winter Stars."

SIGHTSEEING

At the intersection of Krome and Tamiami Trail,
Semi's nudge up against each other by the gas pumps,

The thick rubber of their tires gray with all
The loads they've carried, the roadkill that's pressed

Inside the tread, traces of fur and bone and the smell
Of animal rot, corpse juice and asphalt. At

Miccosukee Casino, the sign's electronic red
"SLOT MACHINES" pulsates high enough to

Be seen above hardwood, miles. The steel pole that
Lifts it is thicker than any tree trunk in the Everglades.

In the banquet hall off the lobby, waiters are dressed
In white shirts and black pants, mostly older men and

Women, their eyes tired from looking at chicken
And peas, *tres leches* for dessert—the casino itself

Is a brown cube projected into the sky, elongated.
A century from now, it will still be here, metal

Windows of the hotel rooms rusting around the edges,
Sawgrass covering the parking lot. A mile and a half

West, there's a prison on the left, quiet fences and
Wire lining the road, surrounding a small lake where no

One fishes. A group of new recruits, corrections officers,
Jog together, making a loop along the tarmac. If you

Keep driving, there's Indian Village and airboat rides
Where they pass out earplugs to dull the noise of

The motor and the fan pushing the flat-bottomed
Machine over wet grass and mud — the tourists

Who sit in the front get splashed with swamp water
And shriek wildly to let everyone know they're

Having a good time. Alligators crawl out of the way.

PRISON WHITE

My classes never start on time. The guards count
Prisoners several times a day and can't get the count right.
So, I wait outside shaded by the overhang from the roof,
The Florida sun hot and yellow as the straight lines my
Students have to follow on the pavement. On top of
A light pole, a crow shouts belligerently, staring
At the foil gum-wrapper a guard just dropped. A librarian
Opens a locked door and lets me in to the classrooms
Through the library—a door that says DO NOT ENTER.
Later, my students are let out from behind the gate and file down
To the education building. We talk about memories, and one,
A Muslim with a skull cap, reads a poem about a woman he knew
When he was outside. I learn some new phrases: the "G-code"
And what it means to "catch a load." He's older now and
Changed, but I notice he doesn't beat himself up about the past
Or preach like the younger guys might. Memories are
There to be honored—fragile things. Last year, one student
Told me he didn't even dream about the outside anymore—
Described himself as "institutionalized." I couldn't say he was
Wrong. He used to talk about how when he was a kid the Miami
Cops would catch him and his friends where they hung out and
Beat them just for the hell of it. He had a lot of anger—no surprise—
But he couldn't write much about it. One time though, he wrote
About making a "stinger" to heat coffee. You take the metal from
A coat hanger and stick one end into an outlet and the other
Into a cup of water. You try not to get shocked in the process.
Maybe he got caught and transferred because I never see him
Around anymore. In the classroom, the fluorescent light
Glares back from walls painted that prison shade of
White mixed with a little blue or green. Somebody
Somewhere must have thought it was relaxing.

Friday

It's late afternoon, and the clouds are
Moving in from the Everglades. Heat
Still clings to the black asphalt and the
Pavement when the first drops break against
The roof. I spent the day teaching down
At the prison in Homestead. There was
No one manning the gate today, and
It was easy to get a parking
Space. For the students, it wasn't so
Easy. Most were late to class. There'd been
Another stabbing in the dorms. A
Thief from one dorm had gone next door. He'd
Stolen there before and must have thought
He could get away with it again.
He didn't. A helicopter came
And airlifted him to Jackson. They're
Good with stab wounds. The guards locked down the
Dorms until they got him out and found
The guy with the knife. He was hiding
In his own dorm. It all took less time
Than you'd think. In class, my students read
Poems they'd written and brought in to
Discuss. We talked about narrative
And how hard it is to make poems
Real. Some of these students are lifers,
But their poems aren't about prison.
They're about memories of a life
Outside, doing coke in a motel
On Biscayne Boulevard, of naked
Girls and air conditioning, of cars
Skidding into canals, heroin,
Dreams that you have over and over
Again. No one mentioned the stabbing.

This Week

One student says, "Inside, you don't have
Friends. You have *associates*. Even
Your best friend will eventually
Betray you." He's done 27
Years already, so I guess he's got
A right to his opinion. He talks
About the gangs the way people on
The outside talk about the weather.
"Wherever you got gangs, they're gonna
Fight over turf." He's one of the ones
Who walk around with a quietness
In their chests. It's almost like they're not
Breathing. They've spent a long time staring
At the linoleum tiles, at the
Electrical outlet where they plug
In the TV, at a copy of
The Qur'an in Arabic. Late at
Night, they may recite a few verses.
If they do, they don't talk about it.
They know when they wake up tomorrow
They'll see the same faces, eat the same
Food, meat that's gone bad, margarine and
Grits. They know what not to think about
As well. One of the quiet ones says,
"Tell me the truth, when you finish here,
Don't you walk a little faster out
That gate than when you were coming in?"
I say, "Yeah, leaving always feels good."

THE MAN ON THE GROUND

In the photograph, the policeman's face
Is paralyzed, lips open, words on the tip

Of his tongue. Because photographs are
Silent, we'll never hear them. His eyes don't

Seem to register what is happening
Around him, the man on the ground, the white

Shirt, the dark stains, the way those arms and legs
Resemble hieroglyphics, the language

Written in Egyptian tombs, spoken by
Dead pharaohs and high priests, embalmers and

Artists. The man on the ground is speaking
With his bent knees and limp elbows, his neck

Turned sideways, his broken glasses staring
At the sun that is not in the picture

But illumines it, light that is present
Everywhere, the same way Goya might have

Painted it, the figures drawn with black lines,
Afternoon shadows, his body become

Image, arms like a broken clock and no face,
The nightstick at the edge of the picture, blurred —

Even as the shutter closes, even
As uniforms shout orders we don't hear,

Can't hear, the man on the ground is speaking.

VI.

Noise of the World

NOISE OF THE WORLD

In the kitchen, the refrigerator fan
Spins softly. Even piles of books
And papers on the dining room
Table seem to be resting. This is
The definition of solitude, the
House that quiet, the dog outside poking
His nose into opossum smells or
The pleasure of rotting leaves. In
The next room, my son is sleeping
Late, as he likes to do. I was the same
Way once. Now, I can't help waking
Early. I make myself coffee and
Eat leftover pita bread with honey.

The news is full of shouting, but
I'm reading it, not listening or
Watching reporters with perfect hair
Try to convey intensity. They're
Right, of course. The news is as bad
As it's ever been, but today something
Feels different. Above the back fence,
The trees are barely moving. They
Listen, in the way trees listen, to the sap
That moves beneath their bark. The
November air has spoken to them
Without words. Their lifespans are
Long; they don't anticipate illness
Or someone with a chainsaw cutting
Them down in pieces—the branches
First, then the trunk. "Future" is
A word too large for comprehension.

We say: "he never saw it coming" and
Feel wiser than whoever didn't see.
The opossums who live under the
Toolshed, though, and the quick rats who

Nest in the palm trees don't divide
Their lives that way, don't sit in the
Morning thinking about history, news,
Politics, about how arbitrarily we
Separate what happened yesterday from
The day before, and how the future always
Ends in chainsaws. But, we're not opossums
Or rats. History is the space we inhabit in
The meantime, the sounds of traffic that
Reach us when the back door is open,
Stories of people who've run out of
Choices, who've become part of the news.

That cup of coffee and the soft, white bread
Depend on being born here, not there. Then,
Not some other time. The refrigerator's
Fan grows louder. An airplane passes
Over the house on its way somewhere
West of here. The dog doesn't even look up.
The tree limbs don't move either. I want
To say this is what matters: solitude, the
Silence of trees and opossums, but it's
Not that easy. The noise of the world
Is always there, even when it's quiet.

*

*When I wrote this last fall, no one
Was dying in my neighborhood except from
Clogged arteries or the occasional cancer.
A few months later, even the light has changed.
Afternoon sun burns through the window
The way kids set ants on fire with a magnifying
Glass, not quite believing their own power.
Today, the streets are quiet everywhere. In
New York, they're burying the dead in mass
Graves, and in Miami we don't know if we're
On the upside or downside of the curve.
Ximena and I wear masks and gloves to go*

To the supermarket, lose count of how many
Times a day we've washed our hands. Last night,
There was no moon. We went for an illegal
Walk through a closed city park, its field
Vacant except for us and a few stars. We were
Afraid to sit on the benches and walked quickly.
There were no passing cars or planes to break
The silence, and we didn't speak.

The lights of the empty YMCA
Seemed possessed of a terrible sadness.

QUARANTINE DAYS

In 1918, my grandfather
Caught Spanish Flu and barricaded
Himself on the sleeping porch before

Collapsing. Later, he agreed to let
In the doctor, but no one else, not
My grandmother, who was pregnant, or

My great-aunt who wasn't married and
Kept house for them. He sweated it out
Shivering, fever waking him up

And then driving him back into sleep.
The night air drifted through the window
Screens. He could hear the neighbors, horses,

Cars rolling noisily down the street.
In the afternoon, sunlight angled
Across his face. He believed he was

Dying, and it seemed better for him
To do that by himself, without the
Disturbance of mourners or people

Fussing over him. But, fate dislikes
That kind of drama, and one day he
Got out of bed, moved the furniture,

And quietly unlocked the porch door.

When I'm at a Loss

Abandoned on an island, Philoctetes still drags
His stinking foot along the sand, fires an arrow at a bird
He can barely see, then crawls over rocks and fallen trees

To pick it up and eat, and Xerxes in some Persian afterlife
Regrets invading Greece. The line between myth and history
Depends on who tells the story. Orpheus is torn apart by maenads,

But his bones continue to sing. Socrates drinks hemlock as
A final lesson to his students. Daedalus builds a labyrinth
To hide the royal offspring, and the screams of sacrificed

Children echo down hallways, along the porticos of temples.
When I'm at a loss, I go back to these stories. I remember
The books where I first read them, the bad illustrations and

Words in large type, my great-aunt's embarrassment
At the violence of Lamb's Shakespeare and her preference
For the Golden Book of the Bible, my own distaste

For the sadness of Anderson, and then the discovery of myth,
Of gods no one I knew believed in, of a wooden horse, and
A parable about a cave, Heracles who strangles snakes

In his cradle, a king who tears out his own eyes, and
A brother and sister who revenge their father's murder.
Outside Ilium, a plague descends on the Greeks,

In Thebes another. Tiresias gives a prophecy no one
Can understand, and in Athens men fight over
Wood to burn the dead.

When I'm at a loss, I return to these stories.

The Day Frank O'Hara Wrote "The Day Lady Died"

I was five years old, and I had scarlet fever,
Lying in my parents' bed because I was sick.
There were pink sheets, and sunlight poured in

Through the curtains. I closed my eyelids. Someone
Had given me Tintin books, and I was waiting
For my aunt to read them to me, waiting to feel

Well enough to walk to the bathroom. The doctor
Stopped by that afternoon to take my temperature
And give me a shot. I looked away and felt the sting.

Thousands of miles north in New York City,
Frank O'Hara was planning to catch a train
To a dinner on Long Island when he saw a picture

Of Billie Holiday on the front page of The New
York Post and realized she was dead. What he
Doesn't say is that he probably still took the train

To that dinner and talked over wine with his hosts
About Picasso or Pasternak, Juan Gris or Melville.
Billie Holiday would have spent that night

In the morgue or a funeral home, no longer herself or
Anyone else, just a voice on the radio or a record player.
More than a dozen years later, I listened to that

Voice, hers, sing "Willow Weep for Me" over and
Over on a scratchy recording, and dozens of
Years after that, I wondered why Frank O'Hara

Bought "a carton of Gauloises" *and* "a carton of
Picayunes," a suicidal combination for sure.
But that night, I didn't know about any of this

Or how hard it is to imagine anyone else's pain.
I just took the aspirins my mother gave me,
Pulled up the covers and went to sleep.

A French Novel

Let me tell you about a book I read in high school.
It begins with a man who's not sure when his mother died.
See, you've already guessed it—set in Algeria

In the years before independence. The man
Has a beautiful girlfriend—at least I remember it
That way—but he doesn't care much about her.

On Sunday, he cooks an omelet on a gas stove
And drinks a glass of wine. Then, he shoots an Arab one day—
I don't think you're supposed to understand why. He

Just keeps talking about the sun as though it were
The reason, but no one can make sense out of that so
He's sentenced to death after witnesses describe

How he didn't cry at his mother's funeral. In high school,
I read he was an existentialist. Looking that up
In the dictionary wasn't a lot of help. Merriam Webster

Defined masturbation back then as "self-abuse."
I did get it, though, that nothing much mattered to him,
And he shouted at a priest at the end. The funny

Thing is that I wanted him to get away, not to
Die in front of the howling crowd he said
He wanted at his execution. The word "anti-hero"

Meant nothing to me. I was fifteen and didn't
Know yet that the world is made up of other people,
That no one's story is separate from anyone else's.

The Arab may have had a sister who'd made dinner
For him, something with chickpeas and spices that
Would go uneaten. And Marie, beautiful Marie,

May have told a friend in a café about how self-absorbed
Meursault had been, what a bad lover, how
He'd never really listened to her, how she planned

To move to Nice someday, open a shop. And,
In the morning after the guillotine, the priest, whose
Name we don't know, may have spooned rose petal

Jam onto a piece of bread, sipped café au lait
From a blue bowl, and thought how lucky he was
Not to be the one who was dead.

IN ANOTHER COUNTRY

In the nightmare of the dark
All the dogs of Europe bark.... — *W. H. Auden*

It was 1939. He'd published "Voltaire at Ferney,"
And war was coming. New York was decorated in
Headlines, each leaked rumor of blockade or invasion
Broadcast from Times Square. Only the gay

Windowless bars were discreet. Freedom was freedom
To be left alone, but only unofficially. Berlin
Had been free once — and look what happened.
He thought by now he would've grown numb,

But hadn't. Letters came, even postcards,
Friends of friends still scrambling to get out. He did what
He could. Washington wouldn't trust the cut
Of his politics. No surprise. They'd left the Spaniards

To anonymous slaughter, and German Jews,
They'd thought, would look out for themselves. Time
Clicked like the meters of taxicabs. At the Automat, a dime
Bought coffee and pie. Too many felt they'd nothing left to lose.

Christopher has gone ahead to California. Hollywood all
Refugees, or so he heard, unemployed for the most part.
The Manns were in New Jersey. Not quite a new start.
He drank at parties and to sleep took phenobarbital.

Old Europe still itched to boil its children, but unlike
Voltaire, he knew his verses wouldn't lower the fire.
The stars here, hard to see at night, flashed no messages to inspire.
On the radio, one too-familiar shout proclaimed a Third Reich.

Across an ocean, Panzer tanks gathered on the Polish frontier.
Soon private life would disappear, antique, odd
As murmuring in Latin on calloused knees to God.
He finished a scotch, uncertain where he'd be in another year.

BRODSKY IN NEW YORK

He would tear the filters off his low-tar cigarettes
And pile them in a pyramid while he smoked. *You must*
Learn to write sonnets, he said, so you can only be
Fooled by someone who can write a better one.
Each class began with writing out from memory
A poem assigned the week before. He paced outside,
Impatient in the hall, while we scratched away trying to get
Each comma right. Then we'd talk, books closed, the
Poem hanging in empty space. *What adjective can you use*
To describe the air? Auden—a stroke of genius—found
"Neutral." We worked through so many poems this way.
What's the best line? Why? Rhymes make a poem
Feel inevitable. The washing machine is an historical
Necessity; poems are not. I asked if rhyme wasn't a trick,
And he said, *Yes, but it's a good one.* Translating Frost
And Donne had kept him alive in prison, in the far north.
He'd been a "social parasite" but almost never mentioned
It. I only remember once, obliquely. I'd made some foolish
Comment about the grave in "Home Burial" and the dirt
Left over from the husband's digging. He looked up from his
Filters and asked if I'd ever dug a grave? Puzzled, not knowing
Where this was headed, I said no. He smiled and replied,
Lucky you.

THE DETENTION CAMP AT PISA, 1943

Pull down thy vanity, I say pull down. – Ezra Pound

He woke at dawn to bugled notes, voices
Shouted on tarmac, his blankets chilled with mist,
And smells of salt and seaweed, Pisan sun.
He'd dreamed of ships sailing the Ligurian Sea
Passages of Vivaldi Olga played.
When they'd arrested him, they called him "Traitor."

Of course, he didn't think himself a traitor,
His thoughts surrounded by a wall of voices,
Confirming this was how the game was played.
Kung understood—his arrow never missed
Its distant target. Tradition was a sea
Filled with gray dolphins leaping beneath the sun.

By noon, he could no longer praise the sun.
He tried recalling if Kung had mentioned traitors;
The Florentine did: Judas, Cassius. See
Inferno XXXIV, and hushed voices,
Lucifer, three-faced, rising from the mist—
And Roosevelt between his teeth—well-played!

The doctors weren't too busy. Two played
Chess in the medical tent. It was the sun,
They said, nerves—Aphrodite in a mist
Retrieving Paris—did that make him a traitor?
Loose canvas flapped in the breeze, the doctors' voices:
"Check!" "Next, I'll take your queen." Goddess from the sea.

His speeches were made on the wrong side of the sea.
His speeches had been recorded, would be played
At trial. Already he could hear the voices.
Il Duce had found the poems "diverting." The sun
Lit up that desk, his outstretched hand. "Traitor"--
He spat at a fly outside his cage and missed.

Evening, shirt soaked with sweat, a rancid mist
Of food smells, excrement, tide pools by the sea.
The war was nonsense. How could he be a traitor?
In Washington, he could explain. Taps played.
Dark now, the moon no substitute for sun.
Dorothy, Olga, the wind—so many voices.

The traitor's vanity dissipates in mist.
At St. Elizabeth's, he voiced the rumbling sea
And played with squirrels and peanuts in the sun.

At Café Versailles

My friend Luis tells me, "All we are
Is memories." We're sitting in the
Back of Café Versailles, the noise
Of plates, silverware, conversations
Ricocheting off the mirrors. I
Think suddenly of those years when my
Mother began to lose remembrance,
Fear my father, believe that gypsies,
Gangsters, even monkeys, were in the
Next room, planning to harm her. At the
Same time, she feared losing him, climbing
Into his bed at the hospital,
Refusing to leave. He was post-op
And hurting. Maybe Luis is right,
And that slideshow with our eyes closed is
All there is, things we thought important
Enough to file away for later.
Even now, so much isn't where it
Should be. I don't remember her voice
Without effort, and I can't be sure
I'm right. Luis says quantum theory
Proves we can't be sure of anything.
I tilt my cup to find the last drip
Of foam from my *cortado*, and I
Disagree, tell him that in this world
People who walk out in the street get
Hit by cars. Movement's predictable.
But, maybe Luis is right. None of
Us seem to be able to predict
Our end. Vallejo excepted—did
He really die on a Thursday in
Paris? I'm not sure. The waiter brings
Our check, and we maneuver between
Tables out to the parking lot. A
Light rain turns the street black and shiny.

TREATMENT

My father had chemotherapy
In the afternoon. I drove him there,
Watched doctors draw off a bag filled
With bloody fluid from his stomach,
Then inject the poison that would keep
Him alive a little longer. He
Was thinner than I'd ever seen him,
Except for his bloated abdomen
That would grow taut, drum-like, a ball of
Pain, until the next week's treatment. It
Was all about dying more slowly,
Clinging to this world he was less a
Part of every morning, coming back
From sleep until the day he wouldn't
Want to come back anymore, see his
Face turning to skull in the mirror—
But even then, he wanted to live.

KITSCH

There were Dresden figurines up on the mantle,
A music teacher despairing at how badly

His students played. The child musicians had
The rosy cheeks you'd expect they'd have

And skin whiter than snow in some remote
European village. Whatever made those fragile

Cheeks rosy, it wasn't blood. Beneath the mantle
Was a gas heater, fireplace without a chimney,

A hissing valve, and a blue flame. It was a damp
Heat, and in winter the air seemed thick and

Hard to breathe. If there was a story behind these
Pasty knick-knacks, I never heard it, but

Someone, probably my mother, must have thought
They were beautiful, inhabiting a world

Pure as mathematics, without insults, rudeness,
Or beatings, a world where nothing breaks,

No one goes hungry, no miscarriages or
Cancers, where the local policeman is a quaint

Old drunk who wags a porcelain finger at
Minor miscreants, where there are no bad

Smells and no one dies in prison. After my
Father's funeral, I sold the figures along

With a large glass pitcher for martinis,
A silver tea set, and the dining room table

That came from a plantation in Mississippi—
They were all kitsch, nothing to do with my

Parents' lives or mine. Today though, I
Watch the usual procession of white clouds

Cross the summer sky and think that if my
Parents were fools to admire these things, then

Socrates was a fool and Plato too. What
Were those Dresden toys but shadow puppets

Cast on the wall of a cave by firelight?

FALLING

None of them are left anymore, the people who
Came to my parents' cocktail parties, the ones

Who drank Wild Turkey on the rocks or Johnny
Walker Red, who mixed ginger ale with whiskey

And told stories I could overhear. Some when they
Fell, made more noise than others, so the whole

Neighborhood knew, but some fell quietly, the way
They wanted to fall, so that almost no one

Noticed they had fallen. Their television sets
Stayed on for days as all the constellations

Swung in the sky as though nothing had happened.

THE REMAINDER TABLE

From the cluttered remainder table,
Cendrars' face, the black-and-white photo
With the gray cigarette ash dangling
Impossibly long from his lips, his eyes
Squinting. You knew he'd been drinking pastis
And stank of tobacco. It was all, I guess,
A cliché, but I wasn't old enough to
Recognize it. I could see him returning
Through cold streets to a cold apartment, his
Bed without company. I didn't know Modigliani's
Portrait, the schoolboy haircut, lips pursed,
Determined, a little cruel. Damaged like
Apollinaire by the war, he saw his lost arm
As a constellation in the night sky. I'm
Quoting what sticks in my memory—how
He knew the sounds of the different trains,
Metal clacking of wheels and track, the
Empty kilometers, telegraph poles on the way
To Vladivostok. He said he was a bad poet
And couldn't go to the end. I didn't know
What *the end* meant when I read that line.
And Jeanne, the prostitute from Montmartre,
Was she really there with him on the train, in
A drafty compartment, or almost asleep
In bed listening to the story? It was a busy time of
Evening. The movie theater across the street
Had just let out. The fluorescent lights overhead
And the bookshelves, cash register, customers,
Myself included, were reflected in the shop window,
Figures in a photograph that was never taken.
For 25 cents, I bought the book.

VALLEJO IN PARIS

He was not yet married to Georgette.
He was on his own, uncertain where he'd sleep or if he'd eat
Before tomorrow. He sauntered nonetheless through galleries,
Staring at paintings, sculptures, while winter turned the sidewalks to ice.
His shoes felt thin, his suit the best he could make of it.
He tried to stay dry and look like he belonged.
If he had conversations with God, who spoke Spanish with a Peruvian accent,
He had them quietly. And, when he could afford it,
Had them over coffee in the cheapest café he could find.
The coffee was cut with chicory, and there was no sugar.
God, he thought, was someone's senile father, seated close to the oven
In a hut in the mountains. The news took a long time to reach him,
And when it did, there was nothing he could do but nod his head, mumbling
"That's too bad. There's so much sorrow there. So much."
The monsters who tore out the intestines of children were real. He'd felt
The damp walls in prison, and he'd seen the glass eyes of the fox and badger
Taxidermied in the ratcatcher's window, their mouths open to show
Their teeth. February rain caused icicles to slide from
The windowsills and smash like empty bottles against the pavement.
He knew it was stupid to argue with God, but he did it anyway,
God who couldn't give him a proper pair of shoes.
He pulled up his collar and stared into the light that shined
Through a restaurant window above the elegant diners
Eating chicken and potatoes.

GHAZAL OF PUEBLA

For Marco Antonio Cerdio Roussell

It's nighttime, and the lights of passing cars flash across tiles
Covering the face of a grand house, a colonial relic of ochre tiles.

On each tile is a blue and white Star of David. In Puebla, the offices
Of the Inquisition were just across the street from these tiles.

Each day, the Dominicans stared at them and cursed, but the owner,
A powerful converso, could afford a house with tiles.

He barred the heavy wooden door against unwelcome visitors.
Only moonlight entered through the windows, between the stars and tiles.

One day they came for the owner, took him in a cart over the mountains
To the capital to be tried and burned. He lost his family, his house, his tiles.

Later, the Dominicans claimed there was a secret synagogue in the house,
But no one knows if that was true. Moonlight still reflects off the tiles.

La Casa de los Azulejos

For Ximena Gómez

Summer's over. It's cool enough now
For the dog to rest outside, the sun
Warming his back, tufts of fur sticking
To the wooden deck. A month ago,
We were in Mexico City. I
Photographed you and Elisa at
The House of Tiles, standing in front of
That picture of Zapata and his
Men having coffee at the counter,
The waitresses dressed like English maids,
The dark hands of the Zapatistas
Curled around white cups, eyes ignoring
The camera. They'd come on horseback—
There's a picture of the horses too.
They were planning to kill Madero,
But Huerta beat them to it. Black and
White photos are all that's left. Six years
Later, Zapata would be dead, his
Body photographed one last time, his
Name written in big white letters on
His chest. Back in Miami, there's not
Much history, at least not like that.
People come here to get away from
History, from revolutions gone
Wrong, from no jobs and little to eat.
The stories here are usually
From somewhere else, Colombia or
Cuba, Peru or Nicaragua,
Stories told on the immigration
Forms you translate, the ones people are
Reluctant to tell. Out back, the sun's
Moved behind the oak trees, and the deck
Planks are a patchwork of thick shadows.
philodendron vines climb up the fence.

SAN ANTONIO
Cali, Colombia

Exhausted after the funeral, we went
To Café Macondo for dinner—sandwiches
And coffee, Coleman Hawkins' "Body and Soul"

Circulating from a speaker, blond teenagers
Speaking Spanish to each other, an older couple
In the corner thumbing a book left on the table,

Science fiction in English. In the front room,
A fan swept the cool night air in from the street.
A small skinny guy with a reflective vest

Patrolled the sidewalk, carrying an iron bar
In the crook of his arm. I couldn't help wondering
If he'd been FARC once—he didn't look

Imposing enough for paramilitary. Or, maybe
He was just a hungry Venezuelan who'd found
A job in the neighborhood. Regardless, I

Wouldn't want to get in his way. Another night,
We came here with friends for dessert, that
White cheesecake topped with *moras,* blackberry

Compote. There are memories you just want to
Rest in for a while. Like this one. It's not
That you forget your losses, but you move them

To the side. They become a frame around the picture,
And the picture surrounds the frame—low,
Whitewashed buildings and narrow streets with

Sidewalks mostly curb, taxis and motorcycles
Accelerating toward clubs, music—salsa or
Reggaeton or the flamenco echoing from a

Restaurant, a blaze of tungsten down the hill,
Where tourists at outside tables cradled beers,
And in the shadows, a heavyset man with a beret

And cane sat each night at the same spot,
Keeping an eye on the parked cars, nodding
To passersby to let them know he's there.

Breaking Curfew

For Ximena Gómez

It's a rainy afternoon in Miami. A lone crow
Calls from a palm tree. The light filtered by clouds
Is so blue that rooftops and fences look like

They're underwater. The dog has no interest
In going outside. After lunch, we worked
On translating your poem, the one about

Bishop Berkeley and how uneasy we can
Become when no one is there to observe us.
You described being alone on a train platform,

And reading it, I was there with you, in a
Moment where we might or might not be real.
These nights when we walk together, the streets

Are empty, the way they are in your poem,
The lights of the shopping mall seem pointless.
I don't know if the department store at the

Corner will ever reopen. From the other side of
The park, it looks like a white church (your phrase)
That no one visits. We stop for a minute to

Look down the canal. Even the ducks have gone.
Only a slick, black surface borders the houses
Like a medieval moat. A few backyard lights

Shine to deter the invaders, who never arrive.
The parking lots are empty. Even the night watchman
No longer makes rounds. I haven't seen his white

Pickup in months. Last night, we heard a car go by,
Playing gospel on the radio. Maybe the rapture
Happened and no one knew it, and we live in

A world God gave up on or, like the Gnostics
Say, turned the job over to someone else. You
Can't tell from these streets. They inspire thoughts

Of abandonment, not comfort. If I saw someone
Walking toward us, you and I would move to
The other side of the street. It doesn't pay to take

Risks. One night a few weeks ago, we saw
The figure of a person sleeping on one of the
Benches in the park. We moved to the banks

Of the canal to avoid him. As far as I know, he
Hasn't been back, and we never see stray dogs
Or cats either. Outside, the afternoon has already

Turned to evening. The sky is a dark blue behind
The darker silhouette of the tree limbs. You used
The word "silhouette" in your poem, and here I am,

Stealing it for mine. I would apologize, but you
Are still busy translating. It'll be time soon to
Make dinner, then perhaps a walk.

April 26, 2020